# WHO STOLE MY BIKE?

## And 20 Other Questions Young Professionals Need to Ask Themselves

by
**David R. McGhee**

Brandon Publishing books may be purchased for educational, business, or sales promotional use. For information, please write: Special Markets Department, Brandon Publishing, P.O. Box 7310, Flint, MI 48507

Unless otherwise stated, scripture is taken from the New King James Version (NKJV), copyright (c) 1979, 1980, 1982, Thomas Nelson, Inc., Publishers.

First Edition

Interior Design by DeMarcus Smith

Cover Design by Chris Watson

ISBN-10: 0988683741

ISBN-13: 978-0-9886837-4-7

*To Kyona, Ryen, Eddie, Paulette, and Brian:*
*I am forever grateful for you.  You all give me permission to be myself.*

*To Grim, Big Dante, Rell, Dame, Sneak, Greg,*
*Lowe, Mouse, Fats, Dallas, Dove, Quincy, KB, VP, GJ, and SJ:*
*I pray my children will one day experience a friendship like ours.*

*Also to my Foss Avenue Baptist Church Family.*

*Lastly, to the entire City of Flint: Act Local, Think Global.*

# CONTENTS

**Foreword**
by
Sylvester Jones, Jr.

## Introduction:

Your state is not your fate

EPILOGUE

**FOREWARD**

Many are said to be leaders, but only a select few are what I would refer to as bold, called leaders. Bold, called leaders aren't necessarily elected or appointed. They are called by the conditions around them, and they lead from where they are. They don't need a title or a position to lead. They only need a cause that is aligned with their convictions and core values. Bold, called leaders don't ask for permission or apologize for standing up for what they believe. They are careful and visionary but they embrace the adage, "If not me then who and if not now, then when?"

Bold, called leaders don't look for awards or accolades. They are simply open to opportunities to make a difference. They are open to opportunities to make life better for others.

Bold, called leaders understand that leaders do what is right no matter who is looking or listening. While they may make mistakes, they operate with an anointing that lends itself to consistency and a general concern for others. Bold, called leaders understand that anger is not passion and celebrity is not leadership. In today's world, bold, called leadership is needed to find solutions to race relations, restore and rebuild families, rebuild and revitalize neighborhoods, and restore order to chaos and protect core values.

It has been said that if you don't stand for something, you will fall for anything. It has also been said that if you don't know where you are going, any road will take you there. David McGhee is a servant-leader who stands for something, and knows where he is going.

More importantly, he is a God-fearing man who lives with a mission to be a voice for the voiceless. I maintain that David McGhee is indeed a bold, called leader.

   -Sylvester Jones, Jr.

**INTRODUCTION**

Before you get started reading, let me set the record straight. I am no millionaire with the secret to success hidden within the pages that follow. Nor am I am a great theologian or Rhodes Scholar who claims to possess a much deeper understanding of the world than anyone else. I am simply a conduit.

I'm writing simply to deliver to you, and to the world, what God delivered to me. Based on my personal and professional experiences, this book is designed to engage, empower and enlighten people while helping them discover the great potential that lies within. Nothing more, nothing less!

This series of questions focuses on life and leadership, birthed from the belief that when approached with logic, many of life's critical issues are tied to a question that follows. Focusing on this fundamental truth, my hope is that you will proclaim your rightful place in your life, your family, your church, and your community. My hope is that this book will encourage you to embrace the person you are, the people around you, and your potential. These foundational principles are at the core of any relationship we have or decision we will ever make. In all we do, it is essential that we take a vital look at the <u>person</u> we are, the <u>people</u> we surround ourselves with, and our God-given <u>potential.</u>

No matter our race, sex, age, background, or religious belief, there comes a time when we each must look within ourselves and develop a personal manifesto to make a difference in our lives. Our future can only be predicted if we create it. Ask yourself these questions and change how your story ends.

We were all born to do something special. We just have to look deep inside ourselves and find out what that something special is.

As humans we are unlike any other species on the planet. Our height, shape, hair color, complexion, personality – everything about us is imperfectly perfect. And we were created for a reason, a cause, and a purpose. The sooner we develop a true understanding of who we are, what we believe in, and what we were born to do, the sooner we'll begin to focus on significance and not success.

Today, more so than ever, many Americans are in situations where they feel stuck. Too often we operate with the mindset, "Oh well, this is just what it's going to be." When we do this, however, we run the risk of never moving forward and thus we believe that our state is indeed our fate. Big mistake! Regardless of our current condition, to accept things as they are creates a stagnant mindset which prevents us from growing.

There is a difference between state and fate. According to Merriam-Webster dictionary, state is a condition or mode of being, as with regard to circumstances. Fate, however, is the supposed force, principle, or power that predetermines events. Fate is the inevitable, final result; the undeniable destiny of what must be. When we accept our state as our fate, and fall victim to our circumstances, we are lying to ourselves. There is a season for everything, which means that no matter what, our current situation will pass. Furthermore, there are times when we must endure the "bad" to position ourselves for the good.

A colleague of mine reminded me of the obvious; a sunrise comes after every sunset, and many rainbows appear after rain falls. In other words, even if we have yet to see the true fruits of our labor – we will in due time.

If we learn anything from movies, we learn that, no matter what the odds are, or how grim the situation may appear, there is always an escape route. All we have to do is just keep going; keep moving forward. We feel, oftentimes, that there's no way out of our current dilemmas because we are easily distracted by distractions. We're focused on why we feel stuck more so than what we can do about it.

In all that we do, perseverance should become one of our closest friends. As you continue to grow, my hope is that you will stay committed to your dreams, never get discouraged, be anxious for nothing, and remain true to yourself. Remember, even if things don't always go the way you plan, your state is not your fate.

# ？
## 1

## WHO STOLE MY BIKE?

**If I can conceive it, and my heart can believe it,
then I can achieve it.**
Muhammed Ali

Believe it or not, Muhammad Ali didn't always grow up with aspirations
of becoming a legendary boxer. It's easy to look at someone who has
been able to become extremely successful and think they've always
had their lives all planned out. This isn't always the case. Trials and
tribulations take root in our lives, and often times they dramatically
change how we thought our story was supposed to end.

As the famous story is told, at the age of 12, Ali had his bicycle
stolen and he wasn't very happy about it. Angry, as any young boy
would be, he reported the missing bicycle to a police officer by the
name of Joe Martin. Ali told Officer Martin that he was going to "whup"
whoever stole his bike. What Ali didn't know at the time, however, was
that Joe Martin was also a boxing trainer. Big surprise! Martin also
told Ali that he "better learn how to box first" before he planned on
attempting to "whup" anyone. This was the beginning.

Martin went on to teach the young Cassius Clay how to box and in a matter of weeks he was training, boxing and winning. This sparked his interest in the sport for which he's so well known. A stolen bike was the key. This was the fuel that drove Muhammad Ali to becoming legendary, and practically dominating the sport of boxing for decades. If you ask any sports fanatic to name their top 5 boxers of all time, I'm certain Ali would be at the top of their list.

And so it is with each of us. Maybe you don't want to be a great boxer, but there is greatness inside of you. This greatness is likely hidden within your passion. We are all passionate about something. In many cases, our passion can be found by honing in on things we are good at, or get excited about. Passion can also be found in our daydreams, or what we find ourselves reading, subconsciously. Passion is that thing that keeps you up at night, and makes you lose sleep. The thing that has the ability to bring you to tears just thinking about it.

A mentor of mine used to say, "The things that tick you off the most are the things you were born to make better." When things tend to bother us, it is often because there is a need – a need that isn't being met -- and we notice it. We notice it because it isn't right, and subconsciously we want to fix it.

The world we live in is full of voids, if you will, that need to be filled. Each of us has something that we can contribute to fill these voids, and our passions can help us accomplish this. Your greatness is linked to your passion. Find that passion by asking yourself, "Who stole my bike?"

### Ask yourself:
What am I passionate about? Where did this passion come from?

(To pen your answer to this question, advance to page 64)

**?**

**2**

---

# WHO AM I?

**You have to leave the city of your comfort and go into
the wilderness of your intuition.  What you'll discover will
be wonderful.  What you discover will be yourself.**
Alan Alda

During this point and time in your life, it is important for you to
understand that you are special and unlike any other person on the
planet.

The gifts that God has given you to share with the world are without
a doubt yours and no one else's.  God has purposely impregnated each
of us - men and women - with things that only we can give birth to.
This may take asking yourself a few key questions.  The most critical of
all, "Who am I?"

No, not what is your name or what school did you go to, or your
place of employment.  But who are you, really?  How would a blind
person know your character?  What do you love to do?  What are you
passionate about?  What dreams do you have?  How do you plan to
leave the world in a better place than you found it?

These may be some questions that you've never asked yourself before. However, remember the words of the old Egyptian novelist Naquib Mahfouz: "You can tell whether a man is clever by his answers. You can tell whether a man is wise by his questions." In many cases, questions are more important than answers.

There was a point in my life where I had to ask myself, "Who am I as a person?" I had to reconcile who I thought I was, how others viewed me, and lastly, but more importantly, what did God have in mind when he created me? I couldn't claim to be one thing, act in a different way, and on the inside be a totally different person. It would be foolish of us to take care of the outside and overlook our inside; our souls, our minds, our thoughts. None of us are perfect, but we must be mindful of the person we are allowing ourselves to become through our daily actions.

One day, following a meeting in which the discussion ended on the topic of popularity, a colleague of mine gave me a sheet of paper. On that sheet of paper read, "Perhaps the most interesting piece of personal advice I ever encountered was this: If you want to be popular, live so that a blind person would like you."

And so it is with each of us. It's easy to interact with, and make a great impression on people we know. But our character and integrity shouldn't end with our peers. This isn't enough. How would you make an impression on someone who couldn't see you, someone who had absolutely no idea who you were? A person who wasn't in tune with your unique style and fashion sense or someone who has no idea how much you paid to get the latest bag, jacket, pair of sneakers.

Lasting popularity (and significance for that matter) doesn't depend upon having good looks or other surface personality traits; but upon inner qualities that somehow communicate themselves to others. Such qualities include care and concern, a friendly voice, a sense of humor, kindness, thoughtfulness, sincere praise, honor, respect, gratitude, encouragement, prayer, faith, and trust in God.  It's tough to become who you desire to become if you don't know who you are right now.

## Ask yourself:

Do I have a clear idea of who I am as a person?  What are some core values I have that define the person I am?

(To pen your answer to this question, advance to page 66)

**3**

---

# PERCEPTION IS REALITY.
# OR IS IT?

**What matters most is how you see yourself.**
Unknown

People will often try to put you in a box. Don't let them. I remember my 4th grade teacher tried doing this to me.

When I was in the fourth grade, I became a man. That sounds crazy, I know. In his own choice words, my 4th grade teacher told me that I wouldn't turn out to be anything. He called me, to my face, an endangered species. True story! At this time, I had no idea what he was talking about.

Basically he was telling me that I had nothing to offer, and that the American dream didn't have a face in it that looked like mine. He was suggesting that I was nothing and would soon become irrelevant to society because I was a young Black male. At that point in my life, I became a man.

I saw him again as a senior in high school, as I was studying one day at the local library with a friend of mine.

We bumped into this teacher and he asked, "What are you doing here?"

"I'm studying", I replied.

"Oh, I thought you'd be a dropout by now," he responded.

With my faith at the forefront, I had to remind myself that this teacher didn't create me. Therefore he couldn't tell me what I would, or would not, turn out to be. And furthermore, his perception of me didn't have to be my reality.

Rick Warren, the world-renowned pastor and writer, once gave this analogy: "If I gave you an invention that you had never seen before, you wouldn't know its purpose, and the invention itself wouldn't be able to tell you either. You would have to do one of two things. Get the owner's manual. Or ask the creator of the invention." This is the only way you can find out its purpose.

Bringing that into reality, my owner's manual was my Bible, and my creator was God. I could care less what other people had to say about me, or what other people thought I would turn out to be. His perception of me was his reality – but it wasn't mine.

Criticism is something we tend to dislike. We feed off of it when it comes to others, but shy away from it when it comes to ourselves. Newspapers, magazine stands, reality television shows, and the like, are filled with disapproval and reproach of others. But if someone criticizes us, we don't want to hear it, read it, or see it. Contrary to popular belief, however, criticism is good. It inspires problem solving and innovation, by forcing us to look at, and do things differently. In many ways, we should actively seek out criticism. General feedback is okay, but only when we are challenged do we become great.

## **Ask yourself:**

How do those who are closest to me perceive me?  Is their perception of me consistent with how I view myself?

(To pen your answer to this question, advance to page 68)

**4**

## AM I PREPARING
## OR REPAIRING?

**By failing to prepare, you are preparing to fail.**
Benjamin Franklin

Many of us are familiar with the phrase "proper preparation prevents poor performance." It has become a staple for many in life and leadership. Very rarely, however, do we actually put this into action. Better yet, I would contend that many of us underestimate the value of preparation.

We live in a reactive culture. Things happen. We react. The problem with this is we don't always respond in very effective ways because we've failed to think about how we would respond. Rarely do we think about the "what ifs?"

It is very detrimental to be so caught up in what is that we don't think about, and prepare for what if? Preparation is what positions us in the right place to achieve our goals. When you are out of position, more bad things happen than good. Preparation is often that thin line between triumph and defeat. We must begin with the end in mind.

This is the power of preparation.

There is no substitute for being prepared. Quite frankly, in preparation we get the most out of ourselves. We study what is, what isn't, and what could be. One must play out various scenarios and then determine, as best as possible, how to respond. If you like sports, imagine this: championships are often won in practice. Think about it.

Becoming the best person you can be is a lifelong process. You reaching your potential won't come by simply graduating from college, or landing a job with a high paying salary. You are becoming the best you, daily.

The power of preparation is plain and clear in our everyday lives. Animals teach us a great lesson in preparation. Their instinct leads them to gather food during the harvest seasons, in order to have something to eat in the winter. The very ground we walk on is carefully prepared by farmers - and nature of course - to grow food. The farmer does his job and nature takes care of the rest. This happens season after season. The rain, snow, sun, and wind all play a part in this preparation.

Here's the bottom line. If you are preparing today, chances are, you will not be repairing tomorrow. This is applicable in business, government, love, leadership, and any other area of our lives. We must all be prepared for that which we cannot avoid.

Imagine yourself living, without limits. Imagine what you are working on will come to pass, and work out in your favor. Prepare yourself for the best, because with preparation, the best is yet to come.

### Ask yourself:

What is one thing I could be preparing for right now?

(To pen your answer to this question, advance to page 70)

@DavidRMcGhee

**?**

**5**

---

## DO I HAVE A PACT?

**For the strength of the pack is the wolf; and the strength of the wolf is the pack.**
Rudyard Kipling

Though we can learn a lot about preparation from animals, as they gather food during the harvest seasons and store it for the winter, there is something that separates us. As humans, the ability to develop long-lasting relationships, and socialize with others, separates us from animals. True friendships are critical to our overall growth and development. Our family members, indeed, play vital roles in our lives. Our friends, however, teach us our most valuable life lessons. Our friends know who we are, and know who we aren't. Our real friends see things in us that we don't even see in ourselves – good and bad. Friendship is a necessity. Especially when we form Pacts!

A Pact can be described as an agreement or a covenant – a step that you take in effort to accomplish a certain goal.

For example, The Three Doctors penned a book titled "The PACT: Three Young Men Make a Promise and Fulfill a Dream". As teenagers, these young men from Newark, N.J., formed a Pact. Their Pact affirmed that they would stick together, go to college, and become doctors – no matter what it took. Through this promise to one another, they did just that. Dr. Jenkins became a professor of dentistry at Columbia; Dr. Hunt became an internist and dean at Princeton; and Dr. Davis became an emergency room physician at two New York area hospitals. All three of these doctors will tell you in a heartbeat that having each other's support helped them get through the tough years, as they pushed themselves to accomplish things no one else in their family had ever done.

In addition, each of them have also ventured into other areas, individually and collectively. They still support each other to this day, and have established The Three Doctors Foundation to encourage the formation of positive peer and mentor relationships.

At this very moment in our lives, God has given all of us a sense of genius and there is no reason why we can't form Pacts of our own – to take us to the next level. Developing a Pact can be very helpful. In 1997, nine of my friends and I began our own Pact. We still stay in touch with, and support one another to this very day. This friendship will last forever, and nothing will ever come between it. We've been through it all together; ups and downs. Our bloodline didn't make us related, but our loyalty to one another still made us family.

So my challenge is that we take the friendships we have one step further and develop Pacts; Pacts that lead toward a common goal, Pacts that will lead us one step closer to being the person God has created us to be.

## Ask yourself:

Who are the five closest people to me?  Are they helping me achieve my goals?

(To pen your answer to this question, advance to page 72)

# ?
## 6

---

## WHOSE SHOULDERS
## CAN I STAND ON?

**They say a midget standing on a giant's shoulders can see much further than the giant.**
Shawn Carter

We've all seen this. You are attending a community rally, a museum, or community parade, and there he is...a father with his son or daughter sitting upon his shoulders. In addition to this being one of the coolest experiences a kid can have, this experience also allows the young person to see things they may have missed had they been on the ground.

As a society, we do a good job at collecting things. As a kid, I collected basketball cards, and when I got older I began to collect sneakers. The tendency to collect things almost seems natural. Think about it.

Sports cards or sneakers may not be your passion. But be it coins, stamps, refrigerator magnets, shot glasses, hand bags, or celebrity hair, there is a good chance that you collect something.

I say this to say, imagine how different our lives would be if we collected people. Yes, people! No, I'm not suggesting that you kidnap people and hide them in your basement. I am insisting, however, that we build strong relationships with others – relationships that can be beneficial to our personal and professional futures. Yes, I am insisting that we collect mentors.

Mentors help guide you in life's journey, showing you the opportunity within the obstacles. Mentors speak up for you and speak out for you, at times when you aren't even around – or can't speak for yourself. Mentors can be found anywhere. When you find one, consider yourself blessed, and make sure you collect him/her.

If you are a person who has never had a mentor, take a moment and think back over your life. There is a good chance that you've probably had one and just didn't know it. During our younger years, our parents and other relatives serve as mentors. As we get older, we tend to look to teachers and sports coaches to fill this role.

As we transition through each stage of our lives, it is important to have people who are right by our side. At one point, our parents are everything to us. They teach us things and provide for us. Though we know they'll always be there for us, as we matriculate into other areas of our lives, we look to others for advice and life lessons. Mom and dad don't teach you everything. Nor will you all of a sudden learn valuable life lessons just by simply growing older. There is a difference between growing old and growing up. We learn from others. Always have, and always will.

While we know that our own education and insights will take us to great heights, having mentors and being able to stand on their shoulders will help us see (achieve) that much more.

## Ask yourself:

Who are my mentors?  Is there anyone who considers me to be their mentor?  If so, who?

(To pen your answer to this question, advance to page 74)

**?**

**7**

---

# DO PEOPLE WANT TO
# CHEAT OFF OF MY PAPER?

**Imitation is the sincerest form of flattery.**
Charles Caleb Colton

Even though I may not know you personally, I am certain that there is something that you can do extremely well. So well that you can teach others to do it! Am I right? What is it? More importantly, what will it be a year from now? What are you committed to mastering by this same time next year? Growth should always be the goal. We should always aim to grow so that we can fully utilize the gifts that God has placed inside of us.

If you are like most people, chances are that at some point in your life, you've cheated off of someone's paper. I know I'm guilty of it. As a matter of fact, when I did happen to cheat (once), I was certain that I was the best cheater any American classroom had ever seen.

I planned ahead and got to class early, being the first student to speak to the teacher – pretending to be well prepared. I even thought to myself, "I'm going to hand my test in first. If I do this, there will be no signs of me cheating." So I thought, until I got caught.

I was scolded three times for cheating. First, I earned an automatic F on the test. Secondly, the school suspended me for my actions. Lastly, my parents lectured me until I fell asleep. What struck me as odd, though, was that all of the focus was on me and what I did. No one seemed to celebrate the victim. Yeah, I said it. No one seemed to celebrate the victim. After all, they were the one doing something right by acing their tests. They've earned the people's trust, by being smart enough to have their work copied. Their previous performance and behavior is noteworthy, and indirectly they are considered leaders within their own right. In other words, just by simply being prepared, studying, and doing the right things, people take notice.

And so it is with each and every one of us. When you do that which you are supposed to do, effectively, you won't be overlooked. People will find a way to be around you, and study your next move. Without saying it, they recognize you as a success – someone they respect.

### Ask yourself:

What is one thing I do well? So well that people come to me, and look to me to get the job done?

(To pen your answer to this question, advance to page 76)

**8**

---

# AM I ROOTING
# FOR THE UNDERDOG?

**There's a place in me that can really relate to being
the underdog.**
Halle Berry

As you support others, make sure you root for the underdog in you. We
go to extreme lengths to cheer on our favorite sports team, or reality
television star, but we miss the boat in giving ourselves the same level
of support for our very own dreams and undertakings.

The underdog is that participant who isn't expected to win. In every
fight, conflict, battle, game, etc., there is an individual(s) who is not
predicted to triumph.

Since the beginning of time, there have always been underdogs.
People know who they are, but they don't receive the same amount
of attention as the favorite. The underdog isn't the first choice for the
record deal, or the shoe contract, or the executive position at the Fortune
500 Company or the CEO seat at the nonprofit organization. They aren't
the political candidate with the most money or influence, nor are they

the sports team with the best win/loss record either. Let's face it. Not many people purchase tickets to see the underdog. Again, people know they exist, but the attention the favorite receives significantly trumps that of the underdog.

Oh, but when the underdog prevails, there is a common resounding theme. "I knew they always had it in them," people will often say. It isn't uncommon for us to want the underdog to prevail. It is uncommon, however, for underdogs to receive the amount of attention they deserve.

In case you aren't fully familiar with it, let me recount the big fight between David and Goliath. During his time, David, a young boy, appeared to have more courage than all of Israel. He approached Saul (the King at the time) and made it known that he wanted to fight Goliath (a big Giant in Israel who scared everyone). At this time, Saul said that David was too young, too weak and too inexperienced to fight this battle.

David, a shepherd, knew a little bit about fighting though. One day as he was tending to his sheep, a lion and bear attacked them, and David was able to fight them off. Going forward, he was intelligent enough to realize that the same God whom saved him from the lion and bear, was the same God that will deliver him from Goliath. David believed in God and he believed in himself, even though he was the underdog.

Regardless of our accomplishments, or lack thereof, each of us has an underdog within us. Find it. Root for it. In due time, it will prevail.

### Ask yourself:

In what area of my life, personal or professional, am I considered an underdog? How have I responded to this?

(To pen your answer to this question, advance to page 78)
@DavidRMcGhee

**?**

**9**

---

# DO I REALLY
# BELIEVE IN MYSELF?

**I am the greatest; I said that even before I knew I was.**
Muhammad Ali

I have what may be some shocking news for you. Are you ready for it?
Here it is: Everybody doesn't believe in you.

I don't say this to be harsh – I say this to be honest. Since this is
the case you must believe in yourself. Believing in oneself has become
underrated in today's society. We live in a culture where, far too often,
we are seeking the approval of others. Often we want this approval
before we decide whether to believe in ourselves, or our ideas.

This happens no matter who you are, or where you are in your life;
personally or professionally. It doesn't matter if you are an honor roll
student or a standout athlete. It doesn't matter if you have the title as
bank president or you work a job as a gas station attendant. It doesn't
matter if you wear nice clothes or drive a nice car. It doesn't even
matter if you have several Facebook friends or thousands of Twitter

followers. None of these things are more important than you believing in you.

In other words, it really doesn't matter who believes in you if you don't believe in yourself. The support of others is always a bonus, but don't let that hold you back from using your ability to make a huge impact in the world. Don't wait for others to approve what God has already promised you.

In many cases, thinking is overrated. Why, you ask? Here's the thing. An athlete plays. A builder builds. An architect draws. A speaker speaks. A leader serves. A writer writes. Get my point?

None of these can be accomplished by simply thinking. If all a writer does is think, the book, movie script, or grant proposal will never come to life. So often in our thinking, we find ourselves wanting to wait for the perfect time to start doing whatever it is we need to, or desire to do. In this case, I encourage you to watch your "wait". The more you wait, the less that gets done.

Nothing is produced through thinking. Sure, thinking is the first step, but acting is the most important. Even if you fail, there is more to learn from starting and failing than there is from just thinking.

You don't need a lot of money to walk into your life's purpose and get started. You don't need the right business partner, a different job title, or the corner office in that Fortune 500 Company. All you need to get started is, you.

### Ask yourself:

What is it that I've been waiting to do? What's holding me back? How could my life be better if I were to just go ahead and get started?

(To pen your answer to this question, advance to page 80)

**?**

**10**

---

## AM I A BURDEN
## OR A BLESSING?

**If you commit to being a blessing for others, God will see fit that you be blessed.**
David McGhee

There is an old African proverb that says: "The prosperity of the trees is the well-being of the birds." To that end, the well-being of those around us and those closest to us speaks to the prosperity of our trees.

As we learn, live, and grow, we develop new relationships, attain more knowledge and perhaps we even make more money than we used to. One may think that as the aforementioned things take place, we are indeed blessed.

This can be tricky, however. So often we get confused into thinking that our blessings come in occupying privilege or position; or by sitting in the lap of luxury and having people cater to us because of the titles we have or the positions we hold in our respective lives. Though we may have these experiences at some point and time, do they really speak to what it truly means to be blessed?

If you talk to a firefighter, for example, I'm sure that he will tell you that when one is asked by the fire chief to do a difficult job or to perform a demanding feat...that person is considered blessed, in a way. Blessed because they are considered trustworthy and able enough to put out that fire or accomplish that particular task. The same goes for many other professions.

This provides, in my opinion, two definitions of the word blessed in this context. One that is based on self and what one is getting or has attained, and the other, based upon what one is giving. Our blessings come in what we've done for others and what we've given.

Each of us has a task, a duty, a mission, a calling, if you will, to be a blessing to others. To that end, there comes a time when each of us will be called to be that blessing, such as the firefighter was.

For our trees to prosper, seeds have to be sown. A good friend of mine always challenges me to do that right thing, no matter what. Integrity reinforcement is what I call it. This approach to integrity is something that I haven't mastered, but I work on it daily and I learn new ways to be the best person I can be. I say this because true learning shouldn't lead to knowledge, alone, but it should lead to action. In other words, we are blessed to be a blessing.

### Ask yourself:

Are there any good seeds that I need to sow? What has prevented me from sowing them? When will I start?

(To pen your answer to this question, advance to page 82)

**?**

**11**

---

# AM I AFRAID OF LIONS, TIGERS, AND BEARS?

**Comfort can often be found in the strangest places.**
David McGhee

No, I'm not referring to the lions, tigers, and bears that Dorothy was speaking of in The Wizard of Oz. No, not the Jazmine Sullivan song either.

The lions and tigers and bears I'm referring to aren't as popular or melodic, but they indeed can provide comfort and soothe the heart and soul such as music does. Aside from the most popular references of the phrase, there is also a concept of lions, tigers and bears that derives from a comic book series. I'm not a fan of comic books, but in working with youth, over the years, you get introduced to new things all of the time.

This comic book series, as strange as it may seem, is very relevant to young people across the country. When put into context, it is actually pretty amazing! Do you remember the childhood fears that were once upon us? Fears such as monsters under the bed...in the closets...

peeking through the windows.

All of us remember the time in our lives, and the lives of others, when there were "monsters under our beds". Monsters so scary that we couldn't sleep in our beds – we insisted on crawling into bed with our parents or those who could protect us. Or at the very least, they had to look under the bed, in the closet, and out of the window and give us that priceless line..."There isn't anything here to get you." Furthermore, during this stage in our lives, we realize the critical role stuffed animals played in our peace of mind.

In this comic book story, a young man by the name of Joey Price realizes that his stuffed animals can actually come to life and protect him; they can guard him from life's monsters that come to get him in the middle of the night. Imagine that! As defenseless as young Joey is, his animals come to his aid.

The author goes on to state:

> A CHILD'S INSTINCTUAL NEED FOR THE COMFORT OF A STUFFED ANIMAL IS ROOTED IN A REALITY LONG FORGOTTEN BY THE ADULT WORLD. THE HIDDEN TRUTH IS THAT THESE COMPANIONS HAVE BEEN DEFENDING CHILDREN SINCE THE DAWN OF TIME. THIS STORY FOLLOWS YOUNG JOEY ON THE ADVENTURE OF A LIFETIME AS HE TRAVELS THROUGH, WHAT THEY CALL IT, THE STUFFED ANIMAL KINGDOM, A JOURNEY THAT PUTS THE FATE OF ALL THE WORLD'S CHILDREN IN HIS HANDS AND BRINGS HIM FACE TO FACE WITH HIS DESTINY.

As we are confronted with "monsters" in our lives, it is critical that we have lions, tigers and bears that can come to our aid. Furthermore, it is imperative that we serve as lions, tigers and bears to others. People should be able to depend on you, and count on you. If they can't count on you they will count you out. Being responsible and accountable are prerequisites to leadership. Why? Because when leaders fail or get derailed, it is often due to them not being responsible or taking full accountability for their actions.

When responsibility and accountability are used as starting blocks, we can travel down any path with our head held high. This is how we truly change the world, and make a difference in the lives of others. Just as young Joey did in the Stuffed Animal Kingdom.

### **Ask yourself:**

Who is depending on me? Am I really being the best person I can be for them?

(To pen your answer to this question, advance to page 84)

**?**

**12**

---

## WHATS IN MY TOOLBOX?

**Give a small boy a hammer, and he will find that everything he encounters needs pounding.**
Abraham Kaplan

I am often reminded of the quote mentioned above. As a kid, my father would let me hang out with him as we worked on his car and other projects in the garage and around the house. Where he was, I was with my toy tool set in hand. Over time I lost piece after piece; losing all except the hammer. I would pound away at any and everything. Besides making lots of noise, however, I really wasn't accomplishing anything.

This in turn begs the question: What's in your toolbox? As we navigate throughout life, yes we will encounter problems – but we must not allow ourselves to hammer away at every issue and expect a sound result. Doing this brings major chaos but minimal change.

If we are to create a better tomorrow for ourselves, and others, we must put the hammer down and reach for other tools in our toolbox. Tomorrow starts today, and it will start with us using a multitude of tools to overcome obstacles that come our way. This is why it is imperative for you to ask yourself the question, "What's in my toolbox?"

If you have a toolbox, great! If you don't have a toolbox, don't worry, we will build one now. Allow me to offer just a few tools to get you going:

**Patience.** You can't argue and have action. Patience is a virtue.

**People.** On your quest to become the best person you can be, make sure you have the right people in your corner.

**Prayer.** You can do this anywhere, and at any time. God is always willing to listen to you.

**Persistence.** Persistent people let nothing stop them.

**Principles.** Develop some core principles for your life and live by them.

**Purpose.** Don't worry about making headlines, just make headway.

**Punctuality.** There is a lot to be said for people who are timely. Great opportunities often come to those who simply show up.

These seven should get you going. You can never have too many tools.

### Ask yourself:
What's in my toolbox? What's missing?

(To pen your answer to this question, advance to page 86)

@DavidRMcGhee

**?**

**13**

---

## IS SUCCESS REALLY
## A GOAL OF MINE?

**The least of things with a meaning is worth more in life
than the greatest of things without it.**
Carl Gustav Jung

Whether you believe this or not, it is said that you will influence at
least 10,000 people during your lifetime. 10,000 people! How will you
use your influence? How will this world be a better place because you
showed up?

Abraham Lincoln overcame many setbacks, and became one of the
most influential presidents, helping to bring about the abolishment of
slavery. Nelson Mandela campaigned for justice and freedom in South
Africa, spending 20 years in jail for his opposition to apartheid. Martin
Luther King, Jr. led the non-violent civil rights movement and inspired
millions to work towards a more equal society. Steve Jobs was a great
visionary, having the largest impact on consumer technology and
mobility that we have ever seen. It has been found that over 50% of US
households own an Apple product. Each of these individuals, along with

countless others, has had an influence on our lives – tremendously. Their success has transformed to significance.

In some area of our lives, we have all experienced a level of success. If you are reading this book, that means you're alive and that, in and of itself, is a blessing and can be looked at as a success. Our lives, however, should be about more than becoming successful. Significance is what we should strive for. Success is too small a word to fulfill what God has placed in each and every one of us.

I look at it like this: Successful people change themselves. Significant people, on the other hand, change the world.

We are living today during a point and time in our nation's history, when people are facing serious barriers. From Wall Street to Main Street, the financial state and economic security of our people stand in peril. People are hurting today like never before. Yet, many of us continue to equate success with money, fancy clothes, big titles, nice cars, and being famous or popular.

Today, success is portrayed as strictly material. Don't get me wrong. There is nothing wrong with having nice things, but the moment we have something that we can't part with, we don't own it – it owns us.

To this end, I would like to offer the same words our 44th president, Barack Obama, offered to a group of students as he addressed them on their day of graduation. "Your appearance should never outweigh your substance, and your celebrity should never outweigh your character."

### Ask yourself:
Have I been focusing on success, alone? What can I do to live a life of significance?

(To pen your answer to this question, advance to page 88)

**?**

**14**

---

# HOW LONG HAVE
# I BEEN IN JAIL?

**The cruelest prison is the one we build for ourselves out of fear and regret.**
Reverend Hill, Warehouse 13

Don't think you're in jail?  Think again!  In some capacity, we all are. The funny thing is, we build these jails ourselves.  In our jail there is a loss of liberty, independence, and even choice.

There is an old fable that tells the story of an eagle who thought he was a chicken:

> THERE ONCE WAS A CHICKEN FARMER WHO FOUND A BEAUTIFUL, LARGE EAGLE'S EGG.  HE PUT IT IN THE NEST OF HIS HEN, ALONG WITH THE OTHER CHICKEN EGGS.  THAT NIGHT THE MOTHER HEN SAT ON ALL THE EGGS, INCLUDING THE EAGLE EGG, AND IN DUE TIME, AN EAGLET HATCHED ALONG WITH A BROOD OF CHICKS.
>
> WHEN THE BABY EAGLE OPENED HIS EYES FOR THE FIRST TIME, IT FIRST SAW THE MOTHER HEN, THUS IDENTIFYING THE HEN AS HIS MOTHER.

The young eagle grew up with all the other chickens. Whatever the chickens did, the eagle also did. He learned to cluck, cackle, and scratch in the dirt for grits and worms. The young eagle thought he was a chicken.

Since the chickens could only fly for a short distance, the eagle also learned to fly just over a short distance. He thought that was what he was supposed to do; so that was all that he thought he could do. And that was all he was able to do. All his life he lived like a chicken.

Years passed and the eagle grew very old.

One day the eagle saw a magnificent bird flying high above him. The old eagle looked up in awe as the majestic bird glided gracefully among the powerful wind currents, with his strong golden wings.

He was very impressed and curious so he asked the hens around him, "Who is that magnificent creature who has so much power and grace and poetry in motion?"

"That is the eagle, the king of the birds," the hens told him, "He belongs to the sky and we belong to the earth because we are mere chickens."

So the eagle lived and died a chicken because that is what he thought he was...

It is natural to look at all of the external things that prevent us from becoming the person we want to be or doing the things we want to do. Yes, things happen that are beyond our control, and that's exactly what they are - beyond our control.  We build a jail for ourselves when we make the mistake of doing the same things today that we did yesterday - never trying anything new.

Our actions define who we are, not our words and more importantly not the words of others.  Our success, joy, happiness, and peace of mind should never depend solely on the actions or words of anyone else.  This jail we build for ourselves is built with bricks of fear, being scared to dream, and the thought that the world won't accept us for simply being ourselves.

God created us all with spiritual gifts that are so special.  To bring these things into fruition, for the betterment of ourselves and others, we must first get out of jail!

## Ask yourself:

What have I done to limit my ability to grow?  Is there anyone else, besides myself, holding me back?

(To pen your answer to this question, advance to page 90)

**?**

**15**

---

## AM I C.O.O.L?

**To be yourself in a world that is constantly trying to make you something else is the greatest accomplishment.**
Ralph Waldo Emerson

As you live, learn, and grow, personally and professionally, it is imperative that you remain C.O.O.L. Ask yourself...

### C

Am I Creative?

I know that sticking to the status quo is very attractive, but that doesn't lead to change. Don't be afraid to be creative in all that you do. Yes, everything! Dig this, there is a huge demand for careers today-jobs that didn't exist 10 years ago. Creativity has, and always will, shape the world. Give it a try, it may shape you too.

### O

Am I Original?

As we live, learn, and lead, we must be original. There is nothing better than being okay with the person God created in us. And, quite frankly, there is nothing worse than pretending to be someone we aren't.

Being original is the only way to be affective, the only way to be genuine, the only way to be...you.

**O**

Am I Obliging?

Obliging is another word for helpful, kind, considerate. One mistake we all make is not always offering the same gestures and respect that we have come to appreciate from others. We want people to be helpful, kind, and considerate toward us; always. We don't wake up thinking, "I hope someone is mean to me today." Yet, we aren't always this considerate toward others. Being obliging, in many respects, is the same as sowing seeds. Without doing this, we don't grow.

**L**

Am I Learning?

Learning isn't just reserved for the brick and mortar of classrooms and universities. There are opportunities to learn all around us. Remember, what we've already learned is one thing. What we haven't learned, however, is a totally different story.

### Ask yourself:

In what ways am I creative, original, obliging, and learning?

(To pen your answer to this question, advance to page 92)

**?**

**16**

---

## DOES GOD CARE ABOUT
## THE SAME THINGS I DO?

**What matters most is a good and ready will to obey God.**
Johannes Tauler

I hoped this question would get your attention. This may be a shock to some, but God really doesn't care about the things we most care about.

I submit to you that we must take a new approach to life – an approach in which we place our focus on making a difference; not simply making a dollar. An approach in which we don't pass what we need, chasing after what we want. An approach in which we forget who we are, and realize who God made us to be.

Regardless of what our role may be to the world, we are all the same in the eyes of God. As we grow personally, professionally, and spiritually, we'll find within us a sense of peace. A sense of peace where the doctor forgets that he is a doctor and the teacher forgets how many degrees she has. The place where the lawyer is not concerned with being a lawyer, nor is the athlete worried about his celebrity or athletic ability. Why? Because, at the end of the day, and since the beginning of time, God really doesn't care about all of these things.

Recognizing this is the true essence of service, which is in turn, the true meaning of life.

I'm no genius, but I truly believe that when our time here on earth is over, and we meet our maker, God doesn't really care about the things that we care about. He won't be concerned with us having the best shoes and clothes. I don't think He will get caught up in how big our house was, where it was located, or the kind of car we drove. It really won't be a concern of His, as to how popular we were and how much money we made.

I truly believe that God's focus can be tied into the famous words of Dr. Martin Luther King, Jr., when he said: "Life's most persistent and urgent question is, What are you doing for others?"

This isn't success, per se, but it is service. And service, my friend, leads to significance.

### Ask yourself:

How have I defined success for my life? Based on the gifts I've been given, how would God describe success for my life?

(To pen your answer to this question, advance to page 94)

**17**

## AM I ORDINARY?

**Don't wait for extraordinary opportunities. Seize common occasions and make them great. Weak men wait for opportunities; strong men make them.**
Orison Swett Marden

Until you believe that you can do extraordinary things, you never will. Not only is it imperative to believe we can do extraordinary things, we must be willing to act and never lose hope, even if things don't always turn out right.

No matter what it is that we strive to be, there is one key ingredient we must embrace. That ingredient: Hope! In this day and age, hope is one of the most important things we can have. To get anywhere in our lives, or become anything, we have to start with hope.

Hope is what made Rosa Parks sit down, so that others could stand up. Hope is what made Fannie Lou Hamer risk her life, in 1964, during the Mississippi Freedom Summer, trying to register as many black voters as she could. Hope is what made Sojourner Truth escape slavery, leaving her infant son.

Only to later take her slave master to court, to win her son back.

Hope is what made a little black boy, with a funny name, grow up and believe he could become president. Hope is the reason you are alive and reading this book today – living off of the prayers of those before us.

On a more personal note, hope is what my grandmother had after I suffered a career ending basketball injury, telling me, "David, you'll do more with your head, than you'll ever do with a basketball."

When we believe in hope, we'll heal our cities. When we believe in hope, we'll heal our states. When we believe in hope, we'll heal our nation. When we believe in hope, then and only then will we be able to "be" anything!

Many of us dream of doing extraordinary things, but deep down inside we don't think we can. Why? Because it's easy to dream, but acting on those dreams and believing in them is a bit difficult. Having a dream isn't that hard, you know! You can fall asleep and have one. Truly believing that you can do that which is extraordinary, however, trumps any dream any day (or night).

It is a crime, in my opinion, to be okay with being ordinary. In fact, ordinary is your enemy. Each and every one of us is uniquely designed to be extraordinary. We are the same, yet so different. No two people walking the face of this earth have fingerprints that are the same. This alone should propel you to embrace your very own uniqueness.

Once you do this, you can see beyond your dreams, and you can see beyond ordinary. It is imperative that you see your future and truly, truly believe in your future. Believe in the extraordinary – for this is how you change the world. No one can make you be an extraordinary person. You have to pull it out of yourself, yourself.

**Ask yourself:**
If I knew I wouldn't fail, what would I do with my life?
What risks would I take?

(To pen your answer to this question, advance to page 96)

**?**

**18**

---

## AM I CURIOUS?

**Intellectual growth should commence at birth and cease only at death.**
Albert Einstein

Some of the world's greatest leaders are also some of the most curious people on the planet. To them, long gone are the days of being satisfied with what they already know. They remain on a hunt to learn things they haven't learned, try things they haven't tried, and also challenge the status quo.

Curiosity is what you often need to discuss the un-discussable, plan the un-planable, and see the often un-seeable. If you can develop the ability to think differently, you will always have a seat at the table.

Curiosity may have killed the cat, but you aren't a cat. With this in mind, I would advise you to hop back on the curiosity train. People who play it safe don't change the world. They just live in it. Big mistake!

How did we get this way? As we get older we tend to think we already know more than we actually do. This in turn causes us to stop asking, searching, and digging deeper for facts and answers.

Curiosity may have been what killed the cat, but it is also what has made men and women great, and it has shaped our world.

How we live, communicate, interact, eat, get from point A to point B, have all been birthed through individuals who were curious. Here are three ways to rediscover the same type of curiosity you may have had as a child:

## Stay open!
The learning process isn't one-fold, it's three-fold: Learning, unlearning, and relearning. Never take things you know (or think you know) for granted.

## Ask! Ask! Ask!
What? Why? When? Who? Where? These should be a regular part of your vocabulary.

## Read outside of your comfort zone!
Your mind isn't limited, so don't limit your mind. Explore new worlds through reading subjects that you aren't normally drawn to. Your mind will surprise you and thank you for it.

## Ask yourself:
In what area of my life (school, work, family etc.) do I need to dig a little deeper, and become more curious?

(To pen your answer to this question, advance to page 98)

**?**

## 19

---

# NO BUSINESS CARD,
# NO SUIT? NO PROBLEM.

**The man who has no imagination has no wings.**
Muhammad Ali

You don't need a set of business cards, or a certain type of clothing to start making a huge impact. Jesus didn't have a business card, or a decorated wardrobe. Yet and still, He is without question the most influential person to ever walk the earth. He saw a void and He filled it. He saw a need, and He met it. He sacrificed His life for the wellbeing of others.

You too have a void in your life that you can fill, or perhaps the life of someone else. You too know a need that needs to be met. You too can do something for the wellbeing of others. Big or small, we all can do something.

Michael Jordan wasn't always the Michael Jordan we know him as today. He did something. Neither was Tim Tebow, Jeremy Lin, Oprah Winfrey, LeBron James, Jay Z, or President Barack Obama. They all did something.

If I said to you, "I have a dream." What's the first thing that would come to your mind? Exactly! Martin Luther King, Jr.

Martin Luther King, Jr. is one of the most notable figures in the world; having a national holiday and a memorable speech. People all across our nation have memorized quotes and speeches from Martin Luther King, Jr. Those four words, "I have a dream", have inspired millions of people to dream of, and strive for a better tomorrow. These four words have been powerful enough to not only inspire people to take action, but this notion has also changed lives. What has been proven true with these words is also true for us as people.

The longer we wait to take control of our life and walk into the destiny that God has for us, the more we blame people for our feeling stuck. The blame game is most convenient for us when we feel stuck. We normally start with blaming the economy, and then we find our way to closer things like our jobs, our boss, and sometimes even our family. None of these are the real issue. If you find yourself blaming others, chances are you are the problem. Not them.

We just have to get started doing something; that something we were wired to do. Great things will happen in our lives, but it isn't always a matter of time. Some things are a matter of choice.

### Ask yourself:
What little thing can I do that will make a big difference
in my life, and the lives of others?

(To pen your answer to this question, advance to page 100)

**?**

---

# AM I ALIGNING
# MY LIFE?

**Lack of direction, not lack of time, is the problem. We all have twenty-four hour days.**
Zig Ziglar

One of the most common mistakes we make is to throw all of our efforts into organizing the things in our lives.  With so many demands on our time, skills, and resources, we often fall victim to the competing voices in our head to organize everything.  The moment we have things just about right, something else is thrown our way, and we find ourselves organizing that right into the middle of what we've just organized.  This leads to chaos, not clarity.

There was one point in my life where I was so busy, that I couldn't get anything done.  I was running from place to place, meeting to meeting, activity to activity, program to program.  I found myself drained at the end of most days, having truly accomplishing very little. I felt as if I was on a treadmill – going nowhere, fast.  It took me a moment to realize it, but I did.

There I was, working as a Program Director for Big Brothers Big Sisters. I was leading a wonderful program. Through my work with the agency, I was able to develop a strong community presence and found myself keynoting an event or receiving an award almost every other month. On the outside looking in, I had it made. The job was great, I had a wonderful boss, and the young people I served were genuine, innocent, youth who simply desired a mentor. I lived and breathed the mission of Big Brothers Big Sisters, and it was evident in my work.

But over time, guess what? I wasn't happy. Ironically enough, the better I became at my role with the agency, the more work I was given. Furthermore, the more I produced the more and more I was trusted with. It was a gift and a curse. Slowly, but surely, I began to get in my own way. So much that I eventually resigned. I ended up firing myself, after seven years. I loved the work, but I felt there was something more God had in store for me to do. Many people thought I was crazy. I walked away from a good paying job on November 15, 2012, with no other job lined up. I now realize, that was the best decision I've ever made.

What we should focus on is aligning our lives, not organizing them. When we align things properly in our lives, we can give the highest level of attention and energy to those things which are consistent with our God-given purpose. We can go from trying to balance our lives, to being okay with our lives being imbalanced, but focused on our strengths. We must reach a point in ourselves where we are okay without being able to do any and everything. Lasting impact comes from aligning our lives, not organizing them.

As one author expresses, attempting to organize things is really no different from being a juggler, and juggling. When we think about it, the core skill of juggling is throwing, not catching. If we spend our lives this way, we'll never have an opportunity to hold onto anything useful, and we'll just wander our way through life. Purposelessly! This isn't good. This is a great way to exist, but not to live.

Aligning your life is way better than organizing it, and you'll have more fun.

### Ask yourself:

In what area is my life out of alignment?
How did things get this way?

(To pen your answer to this question, advance to page 102)

**?**

**21**

---

## WHAT CAN I DO TODAY TO MAKE A DIFFERENCE?

**He who is not courageous enough to take risks will accomplish nothing in life.**
Muhammad Ali

It is known that people create success in their lives by focusing on today. It may sound corny, but today is the only time we have. I've learned that it is too late for yesterday, and I can't depend on tomorrow. This is why today matters.

**Yesterday is gone.** As a matter of fact, it ended last night. Whether good or bad, yesterday is over. If we've had some good days in the past, that's great. Thank God for those days. It would be unproductive, however, to be so caught up on past accomplishments that it hinders us from moving forward. Some people get stuck in the past forever.

Trust me. With years of playing basketball, I know how easy being stuck in yesterday can become. I know people who are still caught up in their glory days, letting their high school basketball careers define them

- exaggerating their abilities as the years pass by. You know what I'm talking about. The older they get, the better they were.

No matter what happened in the past, today is a new day with new possibilities. No matter how much we've accomplished in the past, we cannot move forward off of that alone. We can remember, but we can't think for one second that reminiscing on our past accomplishments will be enough to take us into the future that God has for us. It is impossible to celebrate your way to becoming successful.

**Tomorrow isn't here.** A lot of people think that the future is destined to be bigger and better for them. Sure, that sounds good. But tomorrow is nothing without today's preparation. It's like a farmer expecting his crop to grow without ever planting any seeds. It won't happen! Your future will slowly become your past if you don't prepare for it today.

**Today is more important than you think.** Benjamin Franklin once said "One today is worth two tomorrows." With this in mind, I submit to you that today must not be taken for granted. Our ancestors fought for our today and yet daily, we don't live each day to its fullest potential. In other words, today matters, today is important, today is yours, today is your future.

### Ask yourself:
What can I do, today, to make a difference?

(To pen your answer to this question, advance to page 104)

**E P I L O G U E**

Thank you for taking the time to read this book. My hope and prayer is that it was helpful to you in some capacity; personally and professionally. As a young professional, I am certain that the best is yet to come for you.

You may not believe this, but you were called to be a leader. All of us are.

Too often we believe that leadership is only reserved for those who hold public office, or are in senior management positions. We also make the mistake believing that leadership is some secret place for those of us with extensive resumes, or the church pastor with the largest congregation.

Not true! Anyone can be a leader, and a great leader at that. The fact is, Real Leadership extends beyond a "position" and stretches far and wide into a place where our passions and purpose take the driver's seat.

Below are 3 things (among many) that Real Leaders tend to have in common. I hope you find them useful.

## 1. Real Leaders Focus On Service First

Service is the essence of leadership. The decision to serve first will indirectly bring one to leading. By being a leader who is a servant first, you ensure the needs of others are met. Putting the needs of others first and working toward the common good becomes a priority. This leader doesn't focus on making headlines, they just make headway.

## 2. Real Leaders See What They Look At

There is a difference between looking at something, and seeing it. The decision to truly see what you look at is important. This leader doesn't simply look at something, or someone for that matter. They see, observe, perceive, distinguish, and witness potential. This leader can look at what everyone else looks at, and see something totally different.

## 3. Real Leaders Don't Follow People

Great leaders don't just follow people. Following people only, believe it or not, doesn't lead to success. In addition to having great mentors, knowing who to follow, and when to follow, this leader also has a firm set of principles to follow. This leader knows what he/she stands for because the principles are clear up front and they aren't determined by someone else.

May God continue to bless you, in all that you do. Now go out there and change the world!

-DM

# 21 Affirmations for Young Professionals

1. I will not focus on how much money I make per hour, but more so the value and effort I bring to every hour.

2. I will stay connected to my close family and friends. No amount of success will separate me from them.

3. I know that my alarm clock didn't wake me up this morning. God did.

4. I will know what I stand for before I decide who to stand with.

5. I know that there is too much at stake for me not to follow my dreams.

6. I will always work hard, knowing that some nights will require me to stay awake long enough to make my dreams come true.

7. I will not aim to be famous. I will just do that which deserves to be remembered.

8. I will live with passion and purpose. Always!

9. I will make the right move, at the right moment, with the right motive.

10. I know that there are things I could do, things I want to do, and those things I have to do. I will start with that I have to do.

11. I will commit to my life's purpose. Even if I lose friends, I will never lose focus.

12. I will not run from a challenging task; knowing I will become better because of it.

13. I know that when things aren't going well in my life, personally or professionally, that my state is not my fate.

14. I know that one of the quickest ways to change my life is to change my lifestyle.

15. I will add value to my life, by subtracting the right things.

16. I will be still at times, knowing this is the best way to move forward - reflecting on my past so that I can properly position myself for the future.

17. I will always challenge myself, and challenge the status quo.

18. I know that having morals is better than having money.

19. I know that I was born with special gifts. There are some things that won't be done unless I do them.

20. I will be wise in what I do, for it will soon become what I did.

21. I will never be afraid to be myself.

# Chapter 1
# Who stole my bike?

Ask Yourself:
What am I passionate about? Where did this passion come from?

# Chapter 2
# Who am I?

Ask Yourself:
Do I have a clear idea of who I am as a person?  What are some core values I have that define the person I am?

## Chapter 3
## Perception is reality. Or is it?

Ask Yourself:
How do those who are closest to me perceive me?  Is their perception of
me consistent with how I view myself?

# Chapter 4
# Am I preparing or repairing?

Ask yourself:
What is one thing I could be preparing for right now?

## Chapter 5
## Do I have a Pact?

Ask yourself:
Who are the five closest people to me?
Are they helping me achieve my goals?

# Chapter 6
# Whose shoulders can I stand on?

Ask yourself:
Who are my mentors? Is there anyone who considers me to
be their mentor? If so, who?

# Chapter 7
# Do people want to cheat off of my paper?

Ask yourself:
What is one thing I do well? So well that people come to me, and look to me to get the job done?

# Chapter 8
# Am I rooting for the underdog?

Ask yourself:
In what area of my life, personal or professional, am I considered an underdog?  How have I responded to this?

## Chapter 9
## Do I really believe in myself?

Ask yourself:
What is it that I've been waiting to do?  What's holding me back?  How could my life be better if I were to just go ahead and get started?

# Chapter 10
# Am I a burden or a blessing?

Ask yourself:
Are there any good seeds that I need to sow?  What has prevented me
from sowing them?  When will I start?

## Chapter 11
## Am I afraid of lions, tigers, and bears?

Ask yourself:
Who is depending on me?  Am I really being the best person
I can be for them?

# Chapter 12
# What's in my toolbox?

Ask yourself:
What's in my toolbox?  What's missing?

# Chapter 13
## Is success really a goal of mine?

Ask yourself:
Have I been focusing on success, alone?  What can I do
to live a life of significance?

# Chapter 14
## How long have I been in jail?

Ask yourself:
What have I done to limit my ability to grow?  Is there anyone else, besides myself, holding me back?

# Chapter 15
## Am I C.O.O.L.?

Ask yourself:

In what ways am I creative, original, obliging, and learning?

## Chapter 16
## Does God care about the same things I do?

Ask yourself:
How have I defined success for my life?  Based on the gifts I've been
given, how would God describe success for my life?

# Chapter 17
# Am I ordinary?

Ask yourself:
If I knew I wouldn't fail, what would I do with my life?
What risks would I take?

## Chapter 18
## Am I curious?

Ask yourself:
In what area of my life (school, work, family, etc.) do I need to
dig a little deeper, and become more curious?

## Chapter 19
## No business cards, no suit?  No problem.

Ask yourself:
What little thing can I do that will make a big difference in my life, and the lives of others?

# Chapter 20
# Am I aligning my life?

Ask yourself:

In what area is my life out of alignment?  How did things get this way?

# Chapter 21
# What can I do, today, to make a difference?

Ask yourself:
What can I do, today, to make a difference?

# ABOUT THE AUTHOR

Born and raised in the tough streets of Flint, Michigan, David McGhee sees the world through a unique lens.

As a former program director for Big Brothers Big Sisters, a current professor, and founder of 16th Letter Consulting, a nonprofit and leadership development consulting firm, McGhee has built a strong national reputation as a servant leader who labors diligently to improve the quality of life for marginalized people.

Adept at building key relationships with nonprofit and governmental agencies, David has extensive experience in program development, along with securing local, state, and federal grants. He is also a well-respected, highly sought-after public speaker, recently presenting at TEDxFlint and TEDxDetroit, among others. His work with youth has been widely recognized throughout the country - recently being featured in the September 2012 issue of Black Enterprise Magazine.

David is also a thought-leader, contributing to the National Urban League's 2013 State of Black America Report, Redeem the Dream. His essay, Mentoring Matters: Why Young Professionals and Others Must Mentor, was published alongside essays from other contributors including: Marc H. Morial, Attorney General Eric Holder, Jr., Congressman John Lewis, Rev. Al Sharpton, and many more.

David received his bachelor's degree in public administration & public policy from Oakland University and a master's degree in leadership from Central Michigan University. He can be reached at david@davidmcghee.org.

# REFERENCES

## 1. Who stole my bike?

Opening quote: Muhammad Ali

Ali story: Gregory Allen Howard, a friend of Ali, the award-winning screenwriter of Remember the Titans, The official site of Muhammad Ali, www.ali.com

## 2. Who am I?

Opening quote: Alan Alda

Popularity quote: Meeting at Big Brothers Big Sisters of Greater Flint, 2010

## 3. Perception is reality...or is it?

Opening quote: unknown

Story of teacher: David McGhee and unnamed teacher, Garfield Elementary School, Flint, MI, 1993

Rick Warren Analogy: Warren, R. (2002). The Purpose Driven Life. Zondervan. Grand Rapids, Michigan.

## 4. Am I preparing or repairing?

Opening quote: Benjamin Franklin

Proper preparation quote: unknown

## 5. Do I have a pact?

Opening quote: Rudyard Kipling

The Pact: Hunt, R. , Jenkins, G. & Sampson, D. (2002). The Pact: Three Young Men Make A Promise and Fulfill a Dream. New York, New York. The Berkeley Publishing Group.

## 6. Whose shoulders can I stand on?

Opening quote: Shawn Carter (Jay-Z) Carter, Hovi Baby

## 7. Do people want to cheat off of my paper?

Opening quote: Charles Caleb Colton
Cheating: David McGhee and unnamed teacher and student,
Flint Central High School, 12th Grade

## 8. Am I rooting for the underdog?

Opening quote: Halle Berry
Story of David and Goliath: The Holy Bible: New King James Version (NKJV),
copyright (c) 1979, 1980, 1982, Thomas Nelson, Inc., Publishers.

## 9. Do I really believe in myself?

Opening quote: Muhammad Ali

## 10. Am I a burden or a blessing?

Opening quote: David McGhee
The fire fighter analogy: Adelekan, Tokunbo. (2004). African wisdom: 101
Proverbs from the Motherland. Valley Forge, Pennsylvania. Judson Press.

## 11. Am I afraid of lions, tigers, and bears?

Opening quote: David McGhee
Lions, Tigers, and Bears: Bullock, M (2007) "Lions, Tigers & Bears"
Image Comics.

## 12. What's in my toolbox?

Opening quote: Abraham Kaplan

### 13. Is success really a goal of mine?

Opening quote: Carl Gustav Jung  Influence: unknown
President Barack Obama quote: Arizona State University Commencement
Speech, May 19, 2009

### 14. How long have I been in jail?

Opening quote: Reverend Hill, Warehouse 13
Eagle and chicken fable: Blog, Vikram Karve,  http://creative.sulekha.com/
the-eagle-who-thought-he-was-a-chicken_476479_blog

### 15. Am I C.O.O.L.?

Opening quote: Ralph Waldo Emerson

### 16. Does God care about the same things I do?

Opening quote: Johannes Tauler, German Theologian

### 17. Am I ordinary?

Opening quote: Orison Swett Marden

### 18. Am I curious?

Opening quote: Albert Einstein

### 19. No business cards, no suit?, No problem.

Opening quote: Muhammad Ali

### 20. Am I aligning my life?

Opening quote: Zig Ziglar

### 21. What can I do today, to make a difference?

Opening quote: Muhammad Ali

# 21 Vital Resources for Young Professionals

Big Brothers Big Sisters of America
www.bbbs.org

Bplans
www.bplans.com

Boys & Girls Clubs of America
www.bgca.org

Brewster
www.brewster.com

Echoing Green Foundation
www.echoinggreen.org

Entrepreneur Media Inc.
www.Entrepreneur.com

Evernote
www.evernote.org

Harvard Business Review
www.hbr.org

Inc.
www.inc.com

International Franchise Association
www.franchise.org

KIVA
www.kiva.org

Local Initiatives Support Corporation
www.lisc.org

National Urban League Young
Professionals
www.nulyp.net

ONE
www.one.org

SCORE
www.score.org

Small Business Administration
www.sba.gov

Suze Orman
www.suzeorman.com

The Company Corporation
www.incorporate.com

U.S. Patent and Trademark Office
www.uspto.gov

Young Nonprofit Professionals
Network
www.ynpn.org

Young Entrepreneur
www.youngentrepreneur.com